LEARNING ABOUT ASSESSMENT, LEARNING THROUGH ASSESSMENT

by Mark Driscoll and Deborah Bryant

D1712739

MATHEMATICAL SCIENCES EDUCATION BOARD
CENTER FOR SCIENCE, MATHEMATICS, AND ENGINEERING EDUCATION
NATIONAL RESEARCH COUNCIL

NATIONAL ACADEMY PRESS
Washington, D.C. 1998

NATIONAL ACADEMY PRESS • 2101 Constitution Avenue, NW • Washington, DC 20418

International Standard Book Number 0-309-06133-4

Reviewers

This report has been reviewed by individuals chosen for their diverse perspectives and technical expertise, in accordance with procedures approved by the NRC's Report Review Committee. The purpose of this independent review is to provide candid and critical comments that will assist the authors and the NRC in making the published report as sound as possible and to ensure that the report meets institutional standards for objectivity, evidence, and responsiveness to the study charge. The content of the review comments and draft manuscript remain confidential to protect the integrity of the deliberative process. We wish to thank the following individuals for their participation in the review of this report:

DIANE J. BRIARS
Director, Division of Mathematics,
Pittsburgh Public Schools, Pittsburgh, PA

IRIS R. WEISS
President,
Horizon Research, Inc., Chapel Hill, NC

NORM WEBB
Wisconsin Center for Educational Research,
Madison, WI

LESLIE WILSON
Supervisor of Testing and Training,
Howard County Public School System,
Ellicott City, MD

While the individuals listed above have provided many constructive comments and suggestions, responsibility for the final content of this report rests solely with the authoring committee and the NRC.

Table of Contents

Acknowledgments

We want to take the opportunity to thank the MSEB and Joan Ferrini-Mundy, in particular, for inviting us to write this document. Also, we would like to acknowledge the help we received from numerous colleagues in the preparation of this document, in particular, those who graciously allowed us to interview them and those who read early drafts and gave us critical reviews. These two groups of colleagues include Ann Booth, Diane Briars, Bill Collins, Anne Cummings, Lise Dworkin, Skip Fennell, Susan Loucks-Horsley, Tony Mana, Vance Mills, Jean Moon, Vince O'Connor, Maria Santos, Dan Tobin, De Tonack, Charlie Usher, Norm Webb, and Bob Witte.

Our thanks go as well to the several hundred teachers in the Assessment Communities of Teachers (ACT) Project and Leadership for Urban Mathematics Reform (LUMR) Project, whose dedicated leadership efforts, especially those based on the use of students' mathematical work, have informed us all.

Finally, we would like to acknowledge our EDC colleague, Ruth Leary, for her valuable assistance in preparing the graphics in the document.

Mark Driscoll
Deborah Bryant
Education Development Center, Inc.

Preface

Curriculum reform, performance assessment, standards, portfolios, and high stakes testing—what's next? What does this all mean for me in my classroom? Many teachers have asked such questions since mathematics led the way in setting standards with the publication of the *Curriculum and Evaluation Standards for School Mathematics* (National Council of Teachers of Mathematics [NCTM], 1989). This seminal document and others that followed served as catalysts for mathematics education reform, giving rise to new initiatives related to curriculum, instruction, and assessment over the past decade. In particular, approaches to classroom, school, and district-wide assessment have undergone a variety of changes as educators have sought to link classroom teaching to appropriate assessment opportunities.

Since the publication of *Everybody Counts* (National Research Council [NRC], 1989), the Mathematical Sciences Education Board (MSEB) has dedicated its efforts to the improvement of mathematics education. A national summit on assessment led to the publication of *For Good Measure* (NRC, 1991). This statement of goals and objectives for assessment in mathematics was followed by *Measuring Up* (NRC, 1993a), which provided prototypical fourth-grade performance assessment tasks linked to the goals of the NCTM's *Curriculum and Evaluation Standards*. *Measuring What Counts* (NRC, 1993b) demonstrated the importance of mathematics content, learning, and equity as they relate to assessment. The MSEB is now prepared to present perspectives on issues in mathematics education assessment for those most directly engaged in implementing the reform initiatives on a daily basis—classroom teachers, school principals, supervisors, and others in school-based settings.

The MSEB, with generous support and encouragement from the Carnegie Corporation of New York, seeks to bring discussion of assessment to school- and district-based practitioners through an initiative called Assessment in Practice (AIP). Originally conceived as a series of "next steps" to follow the publication of *Measuring Up* and *For Good Measure*, the project, with assistance from an advisory board, developed a publication agenda to provide support to teachers and others directly involved with the teaching and assessment of children in mathematics classrooms at the elementary, middle, and high school levels.

In a series of three booklets, AIP presents an exploration of issues in assessment. The first booklet, *Learning About Assessment, Learning Through Assessment* discusses ways to assist teachers in learning about assessment and how student work can be a rich resource in professional development. The second, *Assessment in Support of Instruction*, makes a case for aligning assessments with state and district curriculum frameworks and examines ways in which states have shifted their curriculum frameworks and related state assessment programs to reflect the NCTM *Standards* and other perspectives. The third booklet, *Keeping Score*, discusses issues to be considered while developing high quality mathematics assessments. This series is specifically designed to be used at the school and school district level by teachers, principals, supervisors, and measurement specialists.

As we continue in our efforts to understand the implications of standards-based curriculum, instruction, and assessment, it is critical that teachers and others involved with the practice of instruction have the opportunity to reflect on how to best achieve the ultimate goal of improving student learning in mathematics. The MSEB welcomes this opportunity to provide resources in the area of assessment.

Hyman Bass, Chair
Mathematical Sciences Education Board
January, 1998

I.   Introduction

The past decade has seen a growing interest among teachers of mathematics in learning the professional craft of assessment, in order to become knowledgeable about and adept at "the process of gathering evidence about a student's knowledge of, ability to use, and disposition toward mathematics and of making inferences from that evidence for a variety of purposes" (National Council of Teachers of Mathematics [NCTM], 1995).

Major shifts are underway in the world of assessment, which imply increased roles and responsibilities for teachers and motivate teachers' growing interest in assessment. As documented in NCTM's *Assessment Standards for School Mathematics* (NCTM, 1995), there are shifts

- away from basing inferences on single sources of evidence and toward basing inferences on multiple and balanced sources of evidence;

- away from reliance on comparing students' performance with that of other students and toward reliance on comparing students' performance with established criteria;

> Researcher Richard Stiggins and colleagues at the Northwest Regional Educational Laboratory estimate that teachers spend a quarter to a third of their time in efforts to assess students—and their research also shows that on average teachers receive very little support, in preservice or inservice training, in assessment. Stiggins makes a strong argument for bringing teachers and principals together for professional development and cooperative work on strengthening assessment practices. (See Stiggins, 1988.)

- away from relying on outside sources of evidence and toward a balance between these sources and evidence compiled by teachers; and

- away from a preponderance of assessment items that are short, skill-focused, single-answer, and decontextualized, toward a greater use of tasks that are context-based; open to multiple approaches and, in some cases, to multiple solutions; complex in the responses they demand—e.g., in communication, representation, and level of generalization; and drawn from a wide spectrum of mathematics concepts and processes.

The following document addresses professional development that can support teachers in becoming more effective users of assessment. It is based on recent staff-development literature, our own experiences with hundreds of teachers in three national projects (see the Appendix for project descriptions), and the experiences of a group of ten educators we interviewed about their work with teachers in the area of assessment. In the document, we advocate for teachers' professional development in assessment to be carried on with colleagues in groups that work together over time, rather than through a set of disconnected events, a position consistent with that taken by NCTM's *Professional Standards for Teaching Mathematics* (NCTM, 1991). Ongoing collaborative work is particularly desirable because of the critical role in assessment played by drawing and checking inferences that are tied to standards—skills that can facilitate coordinated action among teachers, but require time to develop. However, there are other compelling reasons for teachers to work together on assessment.

1. Assessment has the potential to bring explicit attention to what is important to teach and learn in mathematics. Are students demonstrating that they understand percentage if they can convert a percentage into a decimal? What constitutes a convincing mathematical argument in middle school; in high school? In what ways does algebraic thinking get revealed? Many probing and critical questions like these are at the heart of assessment-focused professional development.

2. Teachers reflecting together on assessment can strengthen classroom assessment and help them calibrate across grades their expectations for mathematics learning outcomes. In particular, individual teachers' observational and questioning skills can be strengthened, as can their capacities to talk with students about progress toward standards. Almost every student of mathematics has had the experience of trying to determine how this year's teacher's values differ from those of last year's teacher. Individual teacher perspectives are important to nurture, but when differing teacher criteria cloud the picture for students as to what is important in

Driscoll and Bryant

mathematical performance, then both learning and performance can suffer.

3. Assessment-based professional development can be a stimulus for teachers to improve their instruction and to change their classroom materials accordingly. Many of the educators we interviewed related versions of the same story from their experience. Over time, when a group of teachers carefully analyze student work and use the evidence to improve classroom instruction, they become clearer and more explicit about the support they need from curricular and instructional programs in their schools and districts. For example, as teachers begin to value the student evidence drawn from using tasks that invite multiple solutions, it is natural for them to develop a desire for curriculum or supplementary materials that will allow them to incorporate such activities regularly into their instruction.

Much of the attention given in the past decade to assessment reform has arisen from the need to end inequities, especially in high-stakes student testing and evaluation. Often, students have been penalized for apparent lack of mathematical understanding when, for example, difficulty with language makes it impossible for them to demonstrate their understanding. Similarly, an important reason to focus on assessment in professional development is to foster equity in learning mathematics—i.e., to increase the chances that each student's mathematical power will be developed to the fullest. Arguably, there will be no real equity until, as part of the fabric of teachers' lives, they work together on regular bases, sharpening their skills in making valid inferences about student evidence to help them identify what appropriate actions are necessary for each student to learn mathematics.

> The reference list for this publication is a good place to start looking for resources.
>
> For mathematical tasks, you may want to explore references 2, 10, 12, 19, 26, 30, 38, and 40;
>
> for scoring rubrics, consider 2, 10, 12, 23, 26, 30, 31, and 42;
>
> for student work samples, consider 2, 10, 12, 26, 29, 31, and 42; and
>
> for descriptions of multiple sources of evidence, consider 12, 19, 23, 28, 29, 30, 40, and 42.

In the sections following this Introduction, we

- cite some of the characteristics and special challenges of assessment-based professional development;

- highlight a set of learning challenges for teachers that have become apparent in assessment-related work, with examples of how these challenges can define the content of teacher work on assessment;

- describe principles that are important in planning and organizing professional development;

- provide a set of sample activities from our own experience in planning and organizing professional development with an assessment focus[1];

- describe a range of teacher concerns about changes in assessment and a framework for understanding and managing the concerns, and apply the framework to the teacher concerns identified in our interviews; and

- make a set of suggestions that we think district and school administrators should heed in order for their teachers to gain the maximum benefit from assessment-focused professional development.

The document is not intended to provide a comprehensive description of the phenomenon that has come to be called "alternative assessment." However, to assist the reader, a number of terms that are used in this document are defined here. (See also NCTM, 1995.) Additional works on alternative assessment are included in the list of references.

- *Classroom assessment* comprises the actions that teachers take (e.g., observations, documentation, quizzes, tests, interviews) to gather evidence in order to monitor progress, diagnose difficulties, assign students to groups, or certify achievement. (See, e.g., Wilson, 1995; Neill, 1995.)

- *Inferences* are conclusions or assertions derived from evidence; deductions. (See, e.g., NCTM, 1995.)

- *Mathematical Power* includes the ability to explore, conjecture, and reason logically; solve nonroutine problems; communicate about and through mathematics; connect ideas within mathematics and between mathematics and other intellectual activities. (See, e.g., NCTM, 1989.)

- A *Performance standard* is a statement of expected performance quality that can be used to make judgments about performances that are central to the curriculum. Performance standards answer the question "How good is good enough?" with performance descriptions and with work samples and commentaries. (See, e.g., New Standards Project, 1995.)

- A *Rubric* is a set of clearly defined rules to give direction to the scoring of assessment tasks or activities. (See, e.g., NRC, 1993b.)

---

[1] It should be noted that the mathematics activities used in this document do not represent the full range of assessment tasks that teachers will need to use. Because we have found that teachers are most challenged by what are termed "alternative assessments," there is a high representation of these in the staff-development activities we describe.

Driscoll and Bryant

II. Learning Challenges

The experience reflected here—the authors' experience and
that of the people interviewed—underscore the centrality of the
assessment process as a guide to design professional development.
Once decisions have been made about the mathematical knowledge and skills that are important to assess, a four-part, cyclical
process is used to monitor the quality of assessment data and decisions. Attending to the process helps ensure that important
knowledge and skills are being assessed (NCTM, 1995).

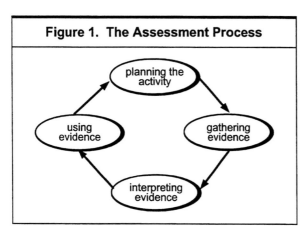

Figure 1. The Assessment Process

Adapted with permission from Assessment Standards for
School Mathematics, *NCTM, 1995, p. 4.*

The assessment process has proved a powerful model for
thinking about student work in mathematics. Used consciously as

a guide to gathering, interpreting, and using evidence, assessment provides a structured way to make values and judgments explicit: What do I think is important for students to learn? What evidence am I going to seek? What meaning do I attach to the evidence I get? How am I going to use the evidence? The assessment process has a simple message about teaching and learning: that a teacher's classroom actions should be based on a thoughtful analysis of student understanding.

Since the introduction of the first set of standards in mathematics in 1989, it has become increasingly evident that, in order to help teachers transform their practice in accordance with standards, professional development must reach levels of need much deeper than the need for information. Working with standards means making decisions that are informed not only by expert information, but also by individual teachers' beliefs, assumptions, and mindsets—all of which affect the interpretation of the information. To be effectively standards-based, therefore, professional

---

Table 1. Seven core learning challenges

Judgment about the quality of mathematics in tasks

Challenge 1. Reaching consensus about quality when looking at mathematics tasks.

Challenge 2. Framing questions and structuring tasks so that what is important and intended is elicited.

Judgment about the appropriateness of tasks

Challenge 3. Aligning classroom assessment with curriculum, instruction, and external assessment.

Challenge 4. Ensuring that tasks involving important mathematics elicit from the broadest range of students what they truly know and can do, and that there are no unnecessary barriers due to wording or context.

Judgment about the quality of student responses

Challenge 5. Deciding what are reasonable student answers to a problem when there is no one "correct" answer.

Challenge 6. Using evidence to make valid inferences about student understanding.

Judgment about consequent actions

Challenge 7. Determining appropriate actions in light of conclusions from student evidence.

development must be rich and complex enough to support teachers at the level of judgment as well as the level of receiving and interpreting information. (See, e.g., Ball, 1994; Little, 1993; Schifter and Fosnot, 1993.)

In this regard, professional development based on assessment is not just about assessment content—e.g., the new terminology, techniques, tasks, etc. Teachers engage with the *process* of assessment, as well. These multiple purposes necessitate more complexity in the design and facilitation of the teachers' learning opportunities, so that they can exercise the judgment and develop the inferencing skills necessary to follow the cycle of the assessment process, from planning to gathering evidence to interpreting evidence to using evidence, and back to further planning. In many assessment work groups, teachers adopt, adapt, and create tasks. As they do so, they are challenged to sharpen and exercise judgment about subject matter, task development, the evidence in student work, and the courses of action implied by student evidence. This section looks at seven core learning challenges we have seen arise in assessment-related professional development. These challenges are organized according the types of professional judgment that teachers may make in response to assessments. (See Table 1 for a summary.)

Judgment about the quality of mathematics in tasks

Though it has not been the norm in staff development to agree on and apply criteria about quality in mathematics, it is difficult to get very deeply into issues of mathematics assessment without being explicit about quality of mathematics tasks and whether a particular task elicits evidence of important mathematical learning.

> *Challenge 1. Reaching consensus about quality when looking at mathematics tasks.*

> *Challenge 2. Framing questions and structuring tasks so that what is important and intended is elicited.*

Ultimately, teachers need to be sure that the tasks they use measure the important mathematics they intend them to measure. This implies some common understanding about mathematical quality. In order for a group of teachers to discuss mathematical quality, there need to be criteria for quality that can be used as dimensions for an informal rating scheme. The point here is not to certify tasks, nor to build an airtight rating scheme. Rather, it is to generate conversations about mathematical quality, so that members of the same teaching community can talk about and listen to opinions about what is important in mathematics.

One option is to focus on the processes involved in doing mathematics. For example, in one teacher-enhancement project[2], teachers took the NCTM definition of Mathematical Power and the language in several of NCTM's curriculum standards related to number sense, and used them to build a rating scheme to rank a cluster of tasks concerned with number sense. (For more information on this process, see Bryant and Driscoll, 1998.)

At a teacher institute for a different project[3], teachers analyzed the following activity using the Mathematical Power definition along with several aspects of algebraic thinking they had been studying, such as *generalizing* and *building rules to represent functional relations.*

> The post office only has stamps of denominations 5 cents and 7 cents. What amounts of postage can you buy? Explain your conclusion. What if the denominations are 3 cents and 5 cents? 15 cents and 18 cents?
>
> What generalizations can you make for stamp denominations m cents and n cents, where m and n are positive integers?

When reporting back on their work, one group showed what they did on the first part of the task (Figure 2). Another group, aiming more at the generalization prompted by the second part of the task, developed an algorithm.

"Given an amount of money, A, we divide it by the smaller denomination. If the remainder is divisible by the difference between the denominations, then we know we can generate the combination using the given denominations. Example: With 5 cent and 7 cent denominations: Try 129. 129 divided by 5 leaves remainder 4. 4 is divisible by 2, the difference between 7 and 5. So 129 works ($5 \times 23 + 7 \times 2 = 129$)."

The mathematical-power lens made it possible to discuss the quality of *mathematical communication* and *reasoning* in each piece and to measure the potential for *conjectures.* Thus, the first group looked at the evidence they had that, in the (5, 7) and (3, 5) cases, they could generate all amounts of postage, after a certain point, while the (15, 18) case had consistent gaps. They conjectured that the concept "relatively prime" is a key differentiating

---

[2]Assessment Communities of Teachers Project, Pittsburgh Public Schools, 1994-1997, supported as a Teacher Enhancement project by the National Science Foundation, ESI-9353622.
[3] Leadership for Urban Mathematics Reform Project, Education Development Center, 1994-1997, supported as a Teacher Enhancement project by the National Science Foundation, ESI-9353449.

Driscoll and Bryant

Figure 2. One solution to the Postage Stamp problem

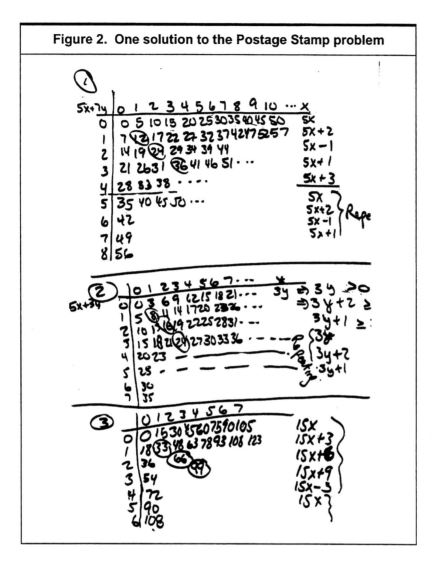

factor. Meanwhile, the second group's reasoning could be analyzed to see why the algorithm worked and whether it could be further generalized.

Other schemes for analyzing an activity are possible, which would offer different criteria for analysis. One possibility is to think of quality in mathematics in light of mathematics as a discipline with tradition. For example, one opinion has been offered that there are three criteria for including a piece of mathematics in the curriculum: beauty, historical significance, and utility (Artin, 1995). (Similarly, Thorpe (1989) suggests as criteria for including topics in the curriculum: i. intrinsic value, ii. pedagogical value, and iii. intrinsic excitement or beauty.) Looking at the postage-stamp problem through such a lens, one could focus on the task's *utility*, not only in its potential to underscore the power of the relation "relatively prime," but also to foreshadow the importance of linear combinations. *Historical significance* could be discussed in several ways, including the overarching topic of Diophantine equations. Finally, *beauty*, which often is experienced when one sees the same concept in different guises, could be discussed in the connection the first group made between the relationship among the rows in the top two tables (captured in their right-hand column) and, respectively, mod 5 and mod 3 systems.

Opportunities to discuss beauty also arise from surprising mathematical results. Groups working on this problem are usually surprised and excited when their evidence leads them to infer that the following statement is true: "For relatively prime stamp denominations p and q, the largest postage amount that *cannot* be made with combinations of p-stamps and q-stamps is $(p-1)(q-1)-1$, or $pq-(p+q)$."

It is not important which particular lens is initially used to discern and discuss the quality of mathematics in a task. It is more important that teachers be afforded opportunities to do mathematics together and to have structured discussions about mathematical quality. Of course, this implies the critical importance of the discussion's facilitator, who must be attentive and prepared, must know the mathematics underlying the tasks, and must be able to introduce relevant viewpoints if they don't arise from the group.

Judgment about the appropriateness of tasks

There are considerable opportunities for teachers to develop their critical skills when weighing the appropriateness of tasks. They can become adept at considering criteria such as student developmental level, available resources and time, and the match between task and purpose. Two particularly important and engaging questions about tasks are whether, as classroom assessments, they are aligned with the curriculum, instruction, and external assessments being used, and how accessible they are to students.

Challenge 3. Aligning classroom assessment with curriculum, instruction, and external assessment.

Challenge 4. Ensuring that tasks involving important mathematics elicit from the broadest range of students what they truly know and can do, and that there are no unnecessary barriers due to wording or context.

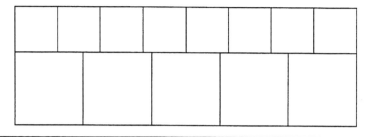

Figure 3. A task on proportion

The small squares are all identical. Their side length is 100 mm. The large squares are also all identical. Show how you can find the side length of a large square without measuring. Give your answer to the nearest millimeter.

Adapted from New Standards Project, 1997.

Regarding these challenges, a central feature of assessment reform in recent years has been the variation of mathematics tasks along multiple dimensions. In creating or adapting tasks along these dimensions, it is of course essential to stay mindful of the quality of the mathematics represented and elicited. It is also important to consider the cognitive demands of a task. Is a particular task intended to gauge how well students have mastered a concept like ratio or proportion? Then its problem-solving demands—the requirements for students to plan and carry out an unfamiliar and complex problem solution—should be minimized. For example, the task in Figure 3, adapted from the New Standards Project (1997), allows students to show understanding of the concept of proportion, without demanding much problem solving.

In contrast, the task below involves problem solving, and also challenges students' conceptual understanding of ratio and proportion.

> Make a two-dimensional paper replica of yourself using measurements of lengths and widths of body parts that are half those of your own body.

An overarching purpose of teacher assessment groups is to help teachers become more knowledgeable about how to select one form of assessment over another. In this case, if a group of teachers is keen to see how well students understand the concepts of ratio and proportion, then they need to consider the following question: Would the problem-solving demands of the second task— e.g., requiring students to make plans and organizing information—provide less valuable evidence of student learning of the relevant concepts than the first task? (For further elaboration on task demands, see Neill, 1995, and Balanced Assessment Project.)

Another issue is the accessibility of the task. For example, as interest in standards-based curriculum, instruction, and assessment has grown in recent years, there has been a shift toward greater use of open assessment tasks and instructional activities. Part of the challenge in aligning curriculum, instruction, and classroom assessment is for teachers to be aware of accessibility issues around openness. Tasks can be open in the front to invite multiple entry points; they can be open in the middle to invite multiple pathways to solution; and they can be open in the end to invite multiple solutions and/or extensions. Beyond certain points, however, tasks can be too open if, instead of aiming the students toward what is important, they make it possible for them to concentrate on form instead of substance, or they make it difficult for students to put their solutions into a broader mathematical framework. Open-ended activities can be seductive, in that a wider range of students can gain access to them and, through the variety of exploration paths, develop a high degree of ownership over their work. However, if a task isn't scaffolded in a way that aims students toward important mathematics, then questions can be asked: "Access to what? Ownership over what?" (For opinions regarding the value as well as risk in using open-ended problems, see, e.g., Clarke, 1993 and Wu, 1994.)

There is yet another task-construction caution regarding accessibility: making sure that no students are unwittingly excluded. Assessment tasks—especially more open tasks—often demand that students interpret wording, context, and diagrams as well as what the purpose of the task is and what is important in the underlying mathematics. In particular, the more open a task and the more context-based it is, the more varied and influential are the assumptions students can bring to their interpretation of the task. A task may allow varying, and even conflicting, assumptions to be brought to bear as students interpret. On their part, task writers assume that students are familiar with certain contexts. In addition, those who use the tasks with students assume the students are aware of their intention in presenting the task.

For instance, in a national teacher project[4] (Driscoll, In preparation), a team of teachers decided to experiment with relevance of context as a dimension in tasks, on the supposition that students are more likely to engage in relevant tasks. Their experiment

---

[4]Classroom Assessment in Mathematics Network Project, Education Development Center, 1991-1993, supported by the Department of Education as a National Eisenhower Project, R168C10098-92.

Figure 4. A task in a new context

DIRECTIONS TO THE STUDENT:
This is an open-ended question. Your answer will be judged on how well you show your understanding of mathematics and on how well you can explain it to others. Please write your response in the space below the question and on the next page, if necessary.

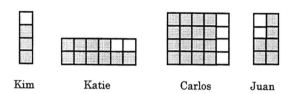

| Kim | Katie | Carlos | Juan |

These are floor plans of four different restaurants. You have been offered a job waiting on tables at these four different restaurants. A recent study shows secondhand smoke from restaurant patrons dramatically increases the risk of lung cancer in restaurant workers. Which restaurant will offer you the least risk? Explain.

(The shaded area represents non-smoking area.)

Adapted from the California Learning Assessment System.

involved taking a task from CLAS, the California Learning Assessment System, and changing the context from a gameboard to the more politically alive topic of smoking in restaurants. (See Figure 4.) The revised task changed the shaded regions in the diagram from gameboard segments to non-smoking areas, and the students were told, "These are floor plans of four different restaurants. You have been offered a job waiting on tables at these four restaurants. A recent study shows secondhand smoke from restaurant patrons dramatically increases the risk of lung cancer in restaurant workers. Which restaurant will offer you the least risk? Explain."

When the teachers gathered the student work on the revised task, they saw evidence that many students thought that it was just as important in the task, if not more important, to analyze room shape for airflow as it was to deal with raw fractional comparisons. Consequently, many strayed considerably in their responses from the mathematical explanations that the teachers wanted to see. In the end, the experiment and, more importantly, the opportunity to analyze the data together, gave the teachers a chance to enhance their appreciation of the importance of wording and context in mathematics-assessment tasks.

The issue of *validity*, which refers to the appropriateness of inferences made from information produced by an assessment, is too complex to cover in detail in this document. But the related question, "Does the assessment tell us what we want to know for each individual student?" is one that deserves careful attention by teachers in professional-development groups, at the very least so they can be more alert to the many non-mathematical factors, like language and culture, that can get in the way of a student's demonstration of mathematical learning.

> "I worry about the language used in how the problem is presented to students, how to make it very clear what they're expected to do, especially if a student is in a testing situation without teacher intervention. I'm concerned with perfecting the skill of making it clear to the student what they are being asked, which is not automatic or easy to do. For example, it's very common that a task ends with 'explain your reasoning' or 'justify your conclusions.' I find that too general for my students, at least until they become acclimatized to the problems." *Interviewed high-school mathematics teacher*

Judgment about the quality of student responses

Among those initiating alternative approaches to mathematics assessment, a frequently recurring realization is that "offering rich problems to students results in getting rich answers. This means that simple marking becomes a thing of the past and that giving students credit for 'the' correct answers becomes a hard job" (Van den Heuvel-Panhuizen, 1994, p. 359). Further, the task may invite a range of mathematical answers. Then it may be more appropriate to ask what is a *reasonable*, rather than correct, answer—reasonable in light of the assumptions that the students bring and reasonable in a mathematical sense.

> *Challenge 5. Deciding what are reasonable student answers to a problem when there is no one "correct" answer.*
>
> *Challenge 6. Using evidence to make valid inferences about student understanding.*

Here, again, open-endedness in a problem can have risks as well as advantages, in particular, if the lines of reasonable expectations for student responses are not clear.

For example, teachers in one project[5] have used versions of the so-called Consecutive Sums task in a range of middle-grades and

---

[5] Leadership for Urban Mathematics Reform Project, Education Development Center, 1994-1997, supported as a Teacher Enhancement project by the National Science Foundation, ESI-9353449.

Driscoll and Bryant

high-school classrooms. In brief, the challenge to students is to investigate which natural numbers can be written as the sum of consecutive natural numbers (e.g., 15 = 7 + 8), and in how many ways (e.g., 15 = 7 + 8 = 4 + 5 + 6), and to explain any patterns and rules that they infer from their investigations. Questions about what are reasonable answers arise in several ways. As a first example, *what is reasonable to expect when students write about the numbers that cannot be expressed as consecutive sums?* Some students merely list the numbers: 1, 2, 4, 8, 16, 32, . . . , in some cases adding the observation that "each one is twice the previous number." Other students will identify the set of "powers of 2." Very few students attempt to prove why powers of 2 cannot be expressed as consecutive sums of natural numbers. Again, teachers grapple with the following question: What is reasonable (and at what age level)?

As a second example, when students offer generalized rules, e.g., regarding the different ways a number can be expressed as a consecutive sum, *what level of explanation is reasonable?* Often, students offer generalizations—sometimes drawing from apparently thoughtful work—with little explanation or convincing argument. (See, e.g., Figure 5.)

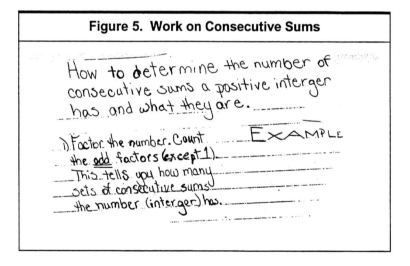

Figure 5. Work on Consecutive Sums

How to determine the number of consecutive sums a positive interger has and what they are.

1) Factor the number. Count the odd factors (except 1). This tells you how many sets of consecutive sums the number (interger) has.

EXAMPLE

It is possible, as we have seen in several projects, to have productive conversations in mixed groups of middle-grades and high-school teachers regarding expectations at different levels for generalization and convincing argument in student work.

Of critical importance is the readiness for unexpected answers on the part of teachers (and others who look at student work). For instance, it is easy to expect that in the following problem, "rule" will elicit from students who have had algebra a response that uses equations and/or standard representations of functional relations.

> *Crossing the River.* Eight adults and two children need to cross a river. A small boat is available that can hold one adult, or one or two children. Everyone can row the boat. How many one-way trips does it take for them all to cross the river? Can you describe how to work it out for 2 children and any number of adults? How does your rule work out for 100 adults?

Even among students who have studied algebra, however, their responses sometimes contain no formal algebra. (Figure 6, for example, shows the entire response of a student.) In various groups of teachers, we have found it advantageous to build a discussion around a question: Though it doesn't look like the "algebraic" response you may have used in doing the task, in what ways is this response still reflective of algebraic thinking?

The learning challenges related to judging the quality of student responses suggest the critical importance of two points of emphasis in discussion: *purpose* and *criteria.* Teacher inferences about quality must be rooted in discussion about purpose in looking at the student work—especially, the distinction between the purpose of understanding student thinking and the purpose of evaluating student achievement. When teachers examine a piece

Figure 6. Work on Crossing the River

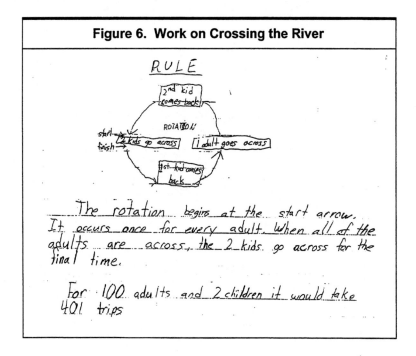

RULE

The rotation begins at the start arrow. It occurs once for every adult. When all of the adults are across, the 2 kids go across for the final time.

For 100 adults and 2 children it would take 401 trips

of student work, there is often an inclination to score it—to decide if the student "got it." But sometimes student work shows signs that, while the student may have *performed* at a low level on a task, he or she is thinking in ways that have great potential.

Teachers working together need the opportunity, for a particular mathematics task, to agree on criteria for what are "reasonable" answers, based on a knowledge of the embedded mathematics and of the developmental levels and experiences of the students, and based on expectations for students' mathematical learning that have been established in the broader contexts in which they teach—in particular, through state and local standards and frameworks (Webb, 1997). In professional-development settings, teachers can hone their skills in making inferences about student thinking, strategize on how to talk with students about standards and their progress toward standards, and discuss how to design instruction to move students' understanding forward. In so doing, they can increase the likelihood that assessment will be used to improve teaching and learning and lessen the chances of individual

---

Figure 7. More work on Consecutive Sums

4. Use the discoveries you made in question #2 to come up with shortcuts for writing the following numbers as the sum of two or more consecutive numbers. Describe the shortcuts you created and tell how you used them to write each of the numbers below as sums of consecutive numbers.

    a) 45   b) 57   c) 62   d) 75   e) 80

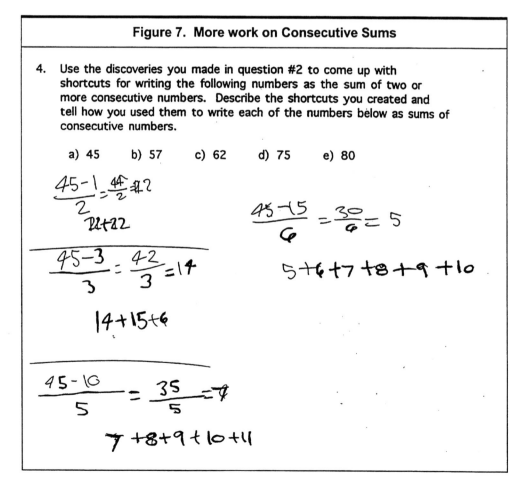

---

teachers wanting to water down assessments because they have concluded their students "can't do this kind of task."

Consider the example in Figure 7, again on Consecutive Sums, in which the student falls well below standards for "describing the shortcuts" and "telling how," but it is easy to infer that there is a well-reasoned procedure underlying the disconnected computations—one that seems based on and works backward from the recognition that three consecutive numbers beginning with n have the sum $3n + 3$; four consecutive numbers have the sum $4n + 6$; five have the sum $5n + 10$; etc.

Not only should teachers agree on criteria, they also should work to calibrate how consistently the criteria are applied across the group. This goal, often referred to as "inter-rater reliability" when the assessment's purpose is evaluation of student achievement, can be accomplished by structuring teacher discussions so that there are frequent opportunities to share, compare, and revise judgments rendered.

Judgment about consequent actions

As mentioned earlier, assessments can be carried out for different purposes. They can aim to inform instruction, or to monitor students' progress toward standards, etc. For each particular purpose, teacher assessment groups can adopt and apply guidelines for what consequent actions should follow their interpretations of student work.

Challenge 7. Determining appropriate actions in light of conclusions from student evidence.

In particular, the enhanced role of teachers in assessment underscores the importance of interpreting student work to craft appropriate classroom responses. Teacher groups can and should learn to analyze a range of student work on a task and to determine points where students need further instruction. Such a process is modeled in the teacher materials from *Exemplars* (1995), as in the example show in Figure 8. The primary-level task is as follows:

Six-Pack of Soda Problem. I often buy cans of soda in a six-pack. If I buy two six-packs of soda each week, how many cans will I buy in a month to recycle? How many six-packs will that be?

Student responses are provided, with commentary from the teacher who submitted the task and student work, which offers interpretations of the student work and so models for teachers how they might analyze similar pieces.

Teacher discussions around this analysis can lead to strategies particular to this student, but also, more generally, they can lead to strategies on how to build student capacities for using procedures and for diagrammatic representation.

Teacher groups that stay together for an extended period will notice in student work some key areas where feedback can affect

---

Figure 8. Student response to the Six-Pack of Soda problem

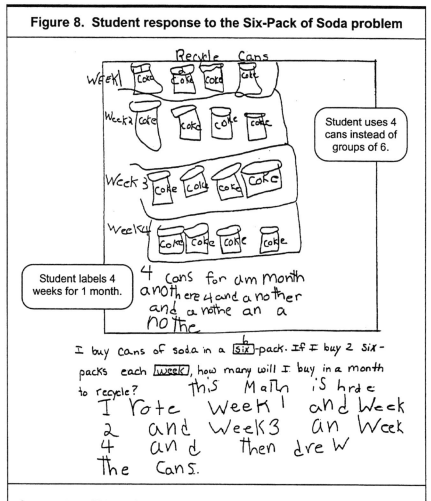

Student uses 4 cans instead of groups of 6.

Student labels 4 weeks for 1 month.

Commentary. This student started to use a helpful mathematical procedure but didn't carry it through. Even though this student has an understanding of the concept of 6, and verbally stated this while using the models provided, s/he did not represent this in the diagram and was unable to get close to a solution.

Reprinted with permission from Exemplars, 1995, p. 9.

Stewart

all squared numbers are the sum of odd numbers because of the picture I made of squared numbers.

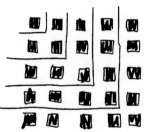

I got the next squared number from 1 by adding 1 and 3 which are odd. Then you add the next odd number 5 and you get the next squared number 9. See how the pattern goes. 16 = 1+3+5+7. Every square will work like that.

Reprinted with permission from Assessment Standards for School Mathematics, *NCTM, 1995, p. 35 and from Ruth Cossey, Mills College.*

students' progress toward standards. For example, many students have difficulty with the notion of mathematical generalization. The excerpt in Figure 9 from NCTM's *Assessment Standards* illustrates, and cites one possible strategy for consequent action. It presents the work of a seventh-grader named Stewart, who summarizes, with diagram and statement, his work with pattern blocks to investigate the different ways to increase the size of geometric figures, like squares.

The text comments, "Stewart has clearly identified a pattern of squared numbers but has not expressed his conjecture, 'All squared numbers are the sum of odd numbers,' precisely. The teacher wrote the following note to Stewart and placed it on his report:

Stewart, your work indicates that you know special odd numbers that sum to 16, 1+3+5+7, not just any odd numbers (e.g., 11+5). You need to be more convincing that your pattern will always work. (NCTM, 1995, p. 35)

Driscoll and Bryant

Most of the mathematics activities in this document, like most of the activities used in our professional-development projects, ask students to construct their responses to mathematical questions. On occasion, however, teachers can benefit from considering the selection, use, and interpretation of more traditional assessments—in particular, multiple-choice items. Discussions about such items can motivate teachers' use of diagnostic questions to uncover patterns of student thinking. For example, the Third National Assessment of Educational Progress presented the following multiple choice item (NAEP, 1983):

> An army bus holds 36 soldiers. If 1,128 soldiers are being bused to their training site, how many buses are needed?

Only 24% of a national sample of 13 year-olds chose the correct answer. A common incorrect choice was a non-whole-number answer, such as one of the representations of 31 1/3, the result of dividing 1,128 by 36. This raises several questions, including: How do students make sense of division-with-remainder story problems? Does the choice of an answer that is not a whole number imply the student is working only in a mathematical domain and not considering the story context? Does choosing the wrong answer mean a student isn't trying to make sense, or is making sense in some alternative way?

It would be shortsighted to conclude that the answers to these questions are the same for all students. One study investigated students' sense making in doing a task similar to the one above. Student interviews "revealed that some students, who would have answered incorrectly if the tasks were presented in a multiple-choice format, were able to offer interesting interpretations of their numerical answers. For example, one student spoke of 'squishing in' the extra students, and others suggested ordering minivans rather than a full bus for the extra students" (Silver et al., 1993, p.120).

There is a critical point here for teachers' professional development. Whether the lens on student understanding is an alternative or traditional assessment, student sense making cannot be presumed. As the responses to the bus item indicate, there are cases where the challenge to teachers is to craft appropriate diagnostic actions to determine how students are thinking.

To a great extent, the learning challenges described in this section define the ground of professional development for teachers as they learn to become more effective users of assessment. We have argued that the professional craft of assessment requires more than acquiring information and how-to knowledge; it requires, as well, the honing and exercise of judgment related to the assessment process: from planning to gathering evidence to interpreting evidence to using evidence for decisions about teaching and learning.

> "But the positive side of that is, they learn more about kids' understanding, more about what they're thinking and not thinking. That's when it becomes assessment that's not separate from instruction, an embedded assessment. Very few people do this or do it well, but when we do it well, if assessment is really part of the instruction, then we don't take it separately and the time spent on it is not a separate issue."
> *Mathematics supervisor of large urban district*

The benefits from these efforts can be considerable. For one, teachers find that assessment and instruction can blend together as mutually supportive endeavors. Second, in embracing the various challenges to judgment around the topic of assessment, teacher groups not only build assessment skills; they can integrate the assessment process into other areas of their professional development, as well. In particular, they can improve the habits and norms of professional discourse, make explicit and sharp the mechanisms for drawing inferences about student learning, and build continuous-learning models within staff-development systems. The next section looks at features of planning, organization, and facilitation that make these outcomes possible.

III. Planning and Organizing Professional Development

This section offers a view of professional development as continuous learning, discusses the role of the facilitator as an advocate for principles of good assessment as well as a supporter of inquiry into teachers' concerns, interests, and learnings, offers a discussion of the features of effective assessment-focused professional development experiences, and provides a suggested core sequence of professional development activities.

As mentioned in the previous section, the assessment process represents a simple message about teaching and learning: that a teacher's classroom actions should be based on a thoughtful analysis of student understanding. There is an analogue for teachers' professional development: that the design and implementation of teachers' learning experiences should reflect a thoughtful analysis of their understanding of the subject matter at hand. By emphasizing the ongoing use of feedback, the 4-part model suggests a way to think of teachers' professional development as a continuous learning cycle, shown in Figure 10 and elaborated below.

> "We found that a supportive environment—where time, professional development, and informal assistance were available to teachers—was an important factor in helping teachers work with the assessment. At such schools, teachers met on a regular basis—during or after school or at professional development sessions—to discuss assessments and instruction" (Khattri et al., 1995).

Plan staff-development events with an eye toward meeting teachers' current learning goals, needs, concerns. As assessment-focused groups develop, perspectives about assessment broaden

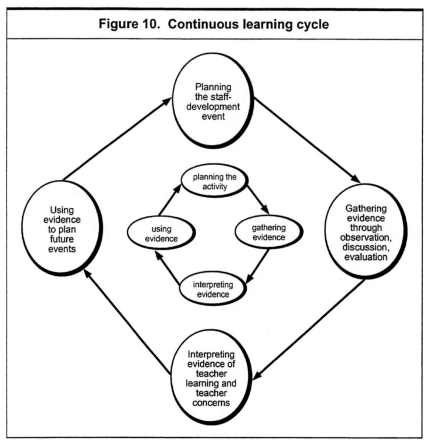

Figure 10. Continuous learning cycle

Planning the staff-development event

planning the activity

Using evidence to plan future events

using evidence

gathering evidence

Gathering evidence through observation, discussion, evaluation

interpreting evidence

Interpreting evidence of teacher learning and teacher concerns

Expanded with permission from Assessment Standards for School Mathematics, *NCTM, 1995, p. 4.*

from attention to testing and grading to seeing assessment as an ongoing process and to considering actions, like the use of open-ended questions, that support both assessment and instruction.

Gather evidence—before, during, and after the event—about teacher learning, through observation, discussion, and written evaluation. The more that staff development allows teachers to experiment actively with assessment, the more accurate will be the appraisal of their learning and their concerns about assessment. Just as the learning of mathematics needs a heavy dose of active investigation by the learner, so too does learning about assessment.

Interpret the evidence to determine what has been learned, and what are lingering or new concerns. As we will explore more deeply in Section VI, concerns about an innovation like alternative assessment change over time and require flexibility and a listening stance on the part of those who plan and deliver professional development. The following are some personal changes we have heard expressed:

"I wanted to see a sampling of new assessments, and now I want to figure out which ones are realistic for me to adopt."

"Now that we know how much our students don't know, what do we do instructionally?"

"I was focused on preparing for the new state test, and now I want to see whether I can use the state scoring guides to improve the quality of my students' explanations."

Use the evidence to chart implications for future staff-development sessions.

This application of the assessment process to teachers' professional development holds value whether the focus of the professional development is assessment or not. However, when the focus is improving the assessment of student learning, with attendant messages about the importance of a standards-based approach to gathering, interpreting, and using evidence, it is especially valuable to model the process for the teachers' own learning.

The role of the facilitator

In the organization of assessment-focused learning experiences, the facilitator has three overarching goals: to identify and *advocate* for what he or she deems important—his/her own interests, values, and beliefs—with regards to principles of good assessment, to *support inquiry* into the interests and concerns of the teachers in the group, and to design effective professional learning experiences that *balance attention to both*.

Advocate for principles of good assessment. An effective facilitator is clear about his or her own interests in leading the group. Is it to raise the quality of mathematics contained in the assessments currently used? Is it to bring coherence to the links among assessment, curriculum, and instruction? Is it to raise awareness about equity issues? To be fully effective, the facilitator needs to be forthright in advocating for these interests. Assessment is all about judgment and values, so there is a natural place in the group for the interests of the facilitator to be expressed and discussed. Several kinds of resources can help facilitators identify and articulate those interests, in particular, the various state frameworks and the several NCTM standards documents.

The NCTM *Assessment Standards for School Mathematics* (1995) is a particularly helpful resource for facilitators: The document outlines six standards for assessment that can support a facilitator in determining what is important to advocate for in mathematics assessment. Below we list the assessment standards, and with each, provide examples of related advocacy statements we have made as facilitators.

- *Mathematics. Assessment should reflect the mathematics that all students need to know and be able to do.* It is not enough for students to find tasks engaging. It is essential that they and their teachers find important mathematical concepts and/or processes through the tasks.

- *Learning. Assessment should enhance mathematics learning.* Students should be able to learn from being assessed. For example, if the focus is making convincing arguments, then they should learn something in the aftermath of the assessment about standards for making convincing arguments.

- *Equity. Assessment should promote equity.* All students deserve regular work on open and challenging tasks.

- *Openness. Assessment should be an open process.* Students need to know what standards they are being held accountable for, and how well they are progressing toward them.

- *Inferences. Assessment should promote valid inferences about mathematics learning.* The processes by which we go from evidence to conclusions about student work need to be explicit.

- *Coherence. Assessment should be a coherent process.* In order for students to succeed in assessment that asks them to construct their own solutions, they need instruction that encourages them to explore and construct their own mathematical meaning for concepts.

Many of the educators we interviewed recommended that facilitators make an early case for the value and importance of teachers becoming more actively involved in improving assessment, in particular, as a way of aligning classroom experience with external assessments. At the same time, honest statements are needed about the challenges inherent in improving assessment.

"I tell the teachers that there are larger shifts happening in the world of assessment, and what we are about to do is meant to be aligned with those shifts. . . . I tell them that working on alternative assessment is 'professional problem solving,' the analogue of what we want students to be doing in the mathematics classroom. Just as we want students to be problem solvers and not just algorithm users, we want teachers to be assessment problem solvers and not just test users. . . . I think it's important to provide examples that can lead to consensus that, under current assessments, we are not getting what we need." *Mathematics supervisor in mid-sized district*

Supporting inquiry. In any given group of teachers, there may be a range of knowledge and experience related to mathematics assessment, thus bringing a range of concerns to the group. It is important for facilitators to elicit the knowledge and the concerns. (Section V describes a framework for identifying and managing

Driscoll and Bryant

such concerns.) Further, at the root of effective assessment change is a careful examination of values, and a determination of what values are shared. Each teacher brings to assessment-based staff development a distinctive set of mindsets, values, opinions, and feelings, often looking very different from—perhaps in conflict with—those held by others. As a consequence, the facilitator needs to infuse a spirit of inquiry into his or her facilitation, and to create the space in which participating teachers can both share their own perspectives and hear the perspectives of others.

Often, when the facilitator successfully inquires into the multiple perspectives of group members, participants discover that the key to addressing individual concerns is to tap into the experience within the group.

"I try to listen to the teachers' concerns. And teachers do start to figure out how to make it reasonable: don't read all 180 papers on a single night, don't read every single journal entry, have kids read one another's papers, have them write group responses. Teachers need to work this stuff out, to develop ways." *Mathematics supervisor of large urban district*

"You need to be practical and reasonable, and to let the teachers know you are. You need to help teachers picture that much of what is 'alternative' builds on what they are already doing. In other words, you need to give credence to informed judgment." *Leader in rural statewide systemic initiative*

One of the assessment leaders we interviewed related: "A good structure will make feedback to teachers a regular feature, so they can mark change and make adjustments. A good structure can magnify and help broadcast small improvements. A good structure can help teachers synthesize the individual achievements of group members, so not everyone has to do everything."

The facilitator's sustained inquiry into the perspectives and concerns of participating teachers creates a public discussion that can shed light both on what is being learned and how the concerns of the group are evolving. This approach provides facilitators the data they need to continue to adapt professional development experiences to best meet the needs of the teacher-learners involved.

Designing professional development to balance attention to both inquiry and advocacy. Facilitation of effective professional development must include both sustained inquiry into participants' perspectives, and advocacy for principles of good assessment. Neither alone is sufficient for good facilitation. The challenge for the facilitator is to bring balanced attention to both. There are several features of professional development that can support facilitators in balancing the two.

Design features of effective professional development

What characterizes groups that productively focus on assessment in their professional development? Below we offer a characterization of design features that, in our experience, contribute to effective assessment-focused professional development. What these design features have in common is that they are consistent with good learning practices and emphasize the importance of the learners' construction of meaning and knowledge: Professional development experiences should be consistent with the kinds of classroom experiences we want for students. Applying the principles of effective learning implies that teachers are provided active-learning opportunities for constructing and testing meaning and for exercising judgment, in particular, in the area of mathematics assessment. (Other useful characterizations of the features of effective professional development include Loucks-Horsley, Stiles, & Hewson, 1996; and NCTM, 1991).

Clarity of outcomes and purposes. Choices made on the content and design of professional development experiences should be consistent with the overall desired outcomes and purposes. The facilitator should be clear about his or her intended outcomes and purposes and communicate these clearly to participating teachers. The facilitator should also seek to understand teachers' expectations for participation in professional development activities.

Ongoing. Professional development should reflect a commitment to continuous learning. Groups that explore assessment together on an ongoing basis, with a clearly defined workscope, can make deeper inroads than groups that meet infrequently or with no clear agendas.

Client-driven and concerns-based. Designers of effective professional development experiences pay close attention to the expressed interests and needs of the participating teachers. Teachers' concerns will vary within the group, and will likely change over time. So facilitators need to be flexible about addressing concerns as they arise (Loucks-Horsley and Stiegelbauer, 1991).

It is often helpful for the facilitator to make regular use of evaluation forms for feedback on professional development sessions. Even a very simple form, consisting of three questions (What did you like about today's session? What do you wish had been done differently? Today's session made me think about . . .) has proved useful for the authors as feedback. However collected, the important points are that facilitators should periodically gather evidence about teachers' concerns, and use that information in planning future professional development experiences. Moreover, facilitators should be explicit about the way they are using this evidence to adjust instruction, to assist teachers in understanding how assessment can be used for this purpose.

Opportunities for developing judgment. Learning experiences should create opportunities, through interaction and discussion among teachers, for addressing the challenges and developing judgment in the areas described earlier in this publication: judgment about the quality of mathematics in tasks, judgment about the appropriateness of tasks, judgment about the quality of student responses, and judgment about consequent actions. Activities such as working on tasks together and discussing the mathematics required by the task, analyzing student work, scoring student work on a rubric, developing rubrics, creating or adapting tasks, and planning diagnostic interventions are examples of such opportunities.

Evidence-based. Learning activities should be based on examining common evidence (e.g., student work, examples of mathematical tasks, case studies) and support discussion of the variety of inferences made from that evidence (Bryant and Driscoll, 1998). The use of common evidence can ground discussion and decision making in the interpretation of data and lessen the risks that decisions will be based on unexamined opinion.

Connected to classroom practice. Professional development experiences should connect to participants' classroom practice in ways that encourage teachers to transfer learning to changes in classroom practice. Connections to practice can be made when, for example, teachers collect and share their own student work, try new tasks and assessment methods in their classrooms, or participate in discussion of classroom-based challenges and concerns.

Opportunities for reflection. Opportunities for individual and group reflection on learning should be provided. Reflection opportunities may include periodic individual reflective writing on selected prompts, sharing reflections verbally in pairs, or teachers creating their own portfolios of work from an ongoing professional development experience.

Collegial. Sessions should be designed to provide the opportunity for participants to learn from one another's perspectives through collegial discussion (Miller, Lord, and Dorney, 1994). Instituting a set of *ground rules* for discussion supports this collegiality, emphasizing the importance of maintaining such habits as listening, expressing concerns openly, and making underlying assumptions clear. Of particular importance in assessment-related professional development are ground rules that guide the ways in which teachers talk about each other's student work. If the work is offered by a teacher for the purpose of analyzing students' mathematical efforts, it is essential that the focus be on the evidence of learning and understanding in the work, and not on the effectiveness of the teacher's instruction. Teachers take risks in offering student work for analysis, and it is important to support them in their risk taking.

Relevant information. Information, including readings and resources such as sample tasks, should be provided to teachers whenever relevant. The references section at the end of this publication can serve as a useful starting point in locating appropriate resources for use with teachers.

Organized to support learning. Professional development experiences should reflect good organizational and logistical practices. For example, materials such as handouts and overhead transparencies should be clear and readable, and should provide adequate information; the room set-up should be conducive to the experience (for example, teachers sitting in groups around tables rather than theater style); and ample time should be provided to accomplish the tasks.

A suggested core sequence of activities

It helps to adopt a core sequence of activities to engage teachers in analyzing tasks and student work. We suggest a sequence below that does just this. Repeated periodically, this sequence can lead to a variety of ancillary activities, and fits nicely within a continuous learning view of professional development. One commonly used core sequence has four steps (see Figure 11), and allows teachers to focus on the challenges named earlier in this document and to develop skills and exercise judgment collegially.

1. The participants investigate several tasks, all similar in content area—e.g., place value, proportional reasoning, or similarity. By *investigate* we mean that teachers do the mathematics themselves as learners.

2. Participants discuss the various opinions in the group regarding what mathematics the tasks are likely to elicit. This supports teachers' exercising of judgment about the quality of the mathematics and the appropriateness of the task for eliciting that mathematics in an equitable and accessible way.

3. On one of the more open-ended tasks, which is deemed accessible to students at all grade levels represented, participants collect student work to be brought to the group.

4. In the group, participants analyze the student work and discuss what kinds of evidence about student understanding are accessible through this task. This conversation supports the

Driscoll and Bryant

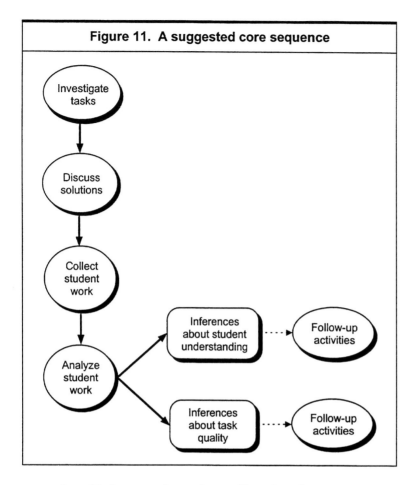

Figure 11. A suggested core sequence

Investigate tasks

Discuss solutions

Collect student work

Analyze student work

Inferences about student understanding — — > Follow-up activities

Inferences about task quality — — > Follow-up activities

exercise of judgment about the quality of student responses and consequent actions. It can also cycle back to the appropriateness of the task in eliciting student responses.

The student-work discussions will lead to inferences about student understanding and/or to inferences about the demand and quality of the tasks. On the basis of these discussions, the group facilitator can suggest some next steps for group activity. For example, if the group discussion leans toward *student understanding*, the group can plan to engage in a variety of activities, such as:

- engaging in case discussions based on instructional dilemmas (e.g., Barnett et al., 1994);

- using performance standards to sort student work for instructional needs; and

- designing or adapting schemes for classroom observation of problem solving.

Alternatively, if the discussion leans toward *task demand and quality*, then the group can plan to engage in activities that cover

- creating tasks that fit the purposes for which they are intended; and

- developing rubrics.

"First start with open-ended problems that the presenter has practiced with, has tried. For newcomers, start with problems that can be completed in one class period. I see too many problems that are problems of the week, that take two or three days to do plus homework, they're too intimidating. Not that they're not useful, just not the best thing for newcomers. They may be more exciting and juicy, but they won't be used as frequently." *High-school mathematics teacher*

Driscoll and Bryant

IV. A Framework for Addressing Concerns

By this point, it should be apparent that there is a particular complexity to assessment-based professional development. Participating teachers learn about new directions in assessment while they engage in repeated applications of the assessment process.

From the start in assessment-focused groups, teachers are challenged to sharpen their skills in gathering and using evidence to make valid inferences. However, the varied underlying concerns that teachers bring to their group work will have a bearing on their attention to the challenges and their capacities to meet the challenges. For example, it would be unwise for a group facilitator to concentrate on teachers' judgment about the appropriateness of tasks if the dominant concern in the group is to get more information about the different kinds of tasks being used in alternative-assessment initiatives.

Those who design assessment working groups need to account for the variety of concerns in their planning. This section describes some common teacher concerns about alternative assessment and a framework to use in listening to and responding to the concerns.

Assuming that there will be a group of teachers working together on assessment, it may be that experience with assessment, and therefore the concerns, will vary within the group. And, no matter what the variation, concerns in a group will change over the course of time. Planning for the group activities needs to take variation and change into account. Whether the driving purpose is to improve classroom instruction or to align what happens in the classroom with externally administered testing, assessment-focused professional development will be experienced by many teachers as an innovation that is nudging, if not requiring, them to change their practice. There is a well-established framework (Loucks-Horsley and Stiegelbauer, 1991) for thinking about the stages of concern that adopters of innovations typically pass through, and that framework, the Concerns-Based Adoption Model (CBAM) is relevant here. Briefly, the framework's stages of concern span transitions from initial awareness of an innovation all the way to exploring how to refocus and improve the innovation. The stages are shown in Table 2.

To capture the flavor of concerns that teachers express about assessment, we interviewed ten people with extensive experience in designing and conducting assessment-focused staff development. The interviews yielded a set of concerns often heard by these group leaders, which we have sorted using the CBAM framework. (See Table 3.) Some of the concerns could sit in more than one category. For example, the bottom, italicized quote seems primarily to be concerned about consequence for the students, but also seems to foreshadow concerns about collaboration with other teachers. No concerns were expressed that seemed to fit under Refocusing. An example of a refocusing concern voiced by teachers once they have worked with innovations in assessment for a while might be, "Will the district support us in using grade-by-grade student work analyses to redefine the district's performance standards?"

Table 2. Stages of concern
Stage 0. *Awareness concerns*: Basic awareness about the innovation.
Stage 1. *Informational concerns*: Focus on learning more detail about the innovation.
Stage 2. *Personal concerns*: Focus on individual's role, the demands of the innovation, and adequacy to meet demands.
Stage 3. *Management concerns*: Focus on efficiency, organization, management, time, best use of resources.
Stage 4. *Consequence concerns*: Focus on impact on students.
Stage 5. *Collaboration concerns*: Coordination and cooperation with others in use of the innovation.
Stage 6. *Refocusing concerns*: Exploration of more powerful alternatives.

From Loucks-Horsley and Stiegelbauer, 1991.

Driscoll and Bryant

Stages 0 and 1. Awareness and informational concerns

How might a group facilitator plan for addressing needs for awareness and information? One economical way is to organize the information around the four shifts in assessment mentioned earlier. These were shifts

- away from basing inferences on single sources of evidence and toward basing inferences on multiple and balanced sources of evidence;

- away from reliance on comparing students' performance with that of other students and toward reliance on comparing students' performance with established criteria;

- away from relying on outside sources of evidence and toward a balance between these sources and evidence compiled by teachers; and

- away from a preponderance of assessment items that are short, skill-focused, single-answer, and decontextualized, toward a greater use of tasks that are context-based; open to multiple approaches and, in some cases, to multiple solutions; complex in the responses they demand—e.g., in communication,

Table 3. Assessment-related concerns	
0. Awareness	
1. Informational	"What are rubrics?" "Portfolios?" "What are examples of the kinds of alternative tasks that are being used?"
2. Personal	"What are the newspapers going to do with the information?" "What conclusions are going to come out of this, and how and where is the information going to be used?" "How do I talk with parents about the changes?" "Will my administrators support me?" "How do I deal with transition? I'm using fewer traditional tests, but don't yet have an adequate system to replace it."
3. Management	"Where can I find the time to fit these tasks in? to score using rubrics? to handle portfolios?" "If a simple grade isn't sufficient, how do I report in a way that is clear, concise, but not backbreaking for me?" "With all the open-ended tasks, how can I be sure what's a right answer?"
4. Consequence	"Will there be some continuity between grades, so that my students don't only see something different in my classroom and not in others?" "Do the new assessments really tell us what we need to know?" "I'm afraid we're de-emphasizing rigor in favor of student inventiveness." "How can you score a piece 'proficient' if the student doesn't get the right answer?"
5. Collaboration	*"Will there be some continuity between grades, so that my students don't only see something different in my classroom and not in others?"*
6. Refocusing	

representation, and level of generalization; and drawn from a wide spectrum of mathematics concepts and processes.

The first implies that attention should be given to defining and providing examples of different sources of evidence—e.g., portfolios, short-answer tasks, performances, student self-assessments, observations. The second implies that attention be given to understanding and reaching consensus about the criteria that are used to judge quality; therefore, examples of scoring rubrics and performance standards need to be provided and discussed. The third implies that information should be provided about efforts in several states and districts to complement test data with other data sources, such as portfolios. The fourth implies that teachers should see and discuss a variety of mathematics tasks.

> "Another question teachers have is, where do the problems come from? Where can I find good performance tasks? What do I do if I don't have one that fits what I'm teaching? Often teachers don't feel they have access to the resources they need. That's the biggest hit in workshops, is giving people collections of problems for them to use as resources in getting started." *District leader of test-change efforts*

Stage 2. Personal concerns

Once concerns for basic information are addressed, and as assessment-focused groups progress, teachers express other, more personal concerns related to the impact on their own experience and on the values they hold dear. The challenges to teachers' judgments about the quality of mathematics, discussed earlier, are particularly likely to raise personal concerns. Understandably, individual feelings of inadequacy about mathematical understandings or skills will raise personal concerns in settings where open discussion is invited and expected.

Drawn from the experience of the educators interviewed for this document, the teachers' expressed concerns reveal a particular set of worries about how vulnerable new assessments will make them. Concerns about support are common, and they include the administrative net underneath, the buy-in by teachers in grades before and after, and the availability of helpful resources. Concerns about smooth transition from an old system to a new one are strongly felt. This is true of individual teachers trying to make changes in their own practice, but it is especially true in settings where widespread assessment change is underway or pending, where concerns include the use of information in and by the community, the handling of community questions, and the use of information to improve programs.

> "Designing alternative forms of assessment is a real tricky thing. If you believe, if you've been convinced, that these forms of as-

sessment are the way to go, then getting the skills to do that kind of assessment is very necessary and requires time. You can't just say, I believe this is a good way to go and so it's going to just happen. We didn't see these forms of assessment when we were in school, we didn't see them in teacher preparation programs, and we haven't ever used them in our classrooms before. Teachers need to not give up when at first an assessment doesn't succeed. A lot of the time, you try something, and it doesn't work at first and it turns out it wasn't assessing what you thought you were assessing. These assessments are new, and different, and teachers ought to have the right to work on it, and improve on it. They need the space to try it without being evaluated on it right away, for instance." *Teacher veteran of portfolio-scoring teams*

"I find it important to talk about taking a long-range view of assessment change. I don't talk about it in the usual one-year time frame, but more in terms of three to five years. I tell teachers, If this stuff is really profound, it may not show up right away." *District associate superintendent*

"Another question teachers have is what are parents going to say, related to how their students will do on standardized tests. If we don't test that way, when students get to standardized tests, how are they going to deal with the multiple choice questions? What if the scores aren't there? These are concerns of both parents and administrators." *High-school mathematics teacher*

"One big question from teachers is, how do we handle concerns and questions from the parents and the community, especially in California or other states where testing is a big political issue?" *Urban district mathematics supervisor*

"My biggest concern right now is how do we educate the public, especially when the assessment is a visible thing. When changes are happening in the classroom, it can be handled, especially through parent-teacher communication: work gets done, feedback is given, work goes home, and there's a gradual awareness that builds." *Urban district mathematics supervisor*

For those facilitating assessment groups, there are a few important considerations in planning to address these personal concerns:

- Provide regular opportunities for participating teachers to discuss their progress and concerns.

- Use small-group explorations of the mathematics, with an emphasis on the building of knowledge in the groups, to alleviate individual feelings of inadequacy around the mathematics.

- Plan to advocate for the longer view in setting the tone with the teachers, to advocate for a commitment to exploration and experiment, and to resist requests to "show us how."

- Find ways to elicit concerns and make them explicit, but be candid and realistic about the possibilities of addressing them within the group.

- Separate the teachers' capacity building—especially the sharpening of judgment about tasks, student work, and consequent actions—from techniques for public relations. The latter may be of interest to participants, but they are no substitute for the former. Give concrete reasons for becoming proficient in assessing students' learning.

- Plan that, over time, the group will select illustrative examples of tasks and student work for purposes of communication about assessment changes. Good examples and informed commentary can be the most effective kind of public relations for assessment in mathematics.

Stage 3. Management concerns

Once teachers invest themselves in trying to incorporate alternative approaches to assessment in their own practice, management concerns arise, related to time management; the application of criteria; and reporting procedures.

> "The question, and I hear this one all the time, is where do you get the time, as a classroom teacher, to score all these papers? And not only to score them, but read them and process what the kids are saying? To be honest, when I was a teacher way back when, most of the time, I'd just check the 'answer column.' I hardly ever looked at the student work. And I think that's what most teachers do. Where do you find the time to read responses, make comments, give feedback? Like using student journals is a terrific idea, but teachers want to know, when am I going to find time to do this?" *Urban district mathematics supervisor*

> "The most frequent question I hear from other teachers is, how is this going to impact everything else I have to do, since this is going to take longer? . . . The big issue is time, and time in the perspective of, if I spend time on this stuff, how am I going to be able to cover the curriculum? . . . The time issue usually comes up in terms of the coverage of the curriculum. And I usually have to answer that by saying, ultimately we're going to have to grab stuff out of the curriculum. Because it's a legitimate concern, how can you do this stuff, and still cover the same curriculum." *High-school mathematics teacher*

In our experience and in the experience of those we consulted, one of the most effective ways to address management concerns, once they have been elicited, is to ask teachers to address the group who have found ways to address particular management concerns. This approach increases the number of effective strategies available to the group, going beyond the personal experience of the facilitator.

Driscoll and Bryant

In addition, there are helpful print resources available, such as Petit (1992), Stenmark (1991), and Tsuruda (1994).

Stages 4 and 5. Consequence and collaboration concerns

Even as they grapple with management concerns, teachers who are invested in learning through assessment and adopting alternative approaches to assessment develop concerns related to how their changes in assessment will affect the quality of their classroom work and the learning of their students. Two prominent clusters of such concerns are content and equity.

Content. An essential component of learning through assessment is exposure to a variety of mathematics tasks. As they become familiar with tasks that require student performance, or that are open or complex, teachers often express concerns about validity, rigor, and quality.

> "As we move to using new forms of assessment, the question I hear most often from teachers, and from parents, is 'Where's the math?' I think people can often see how these open-ended problems do address the first four NCTM standards: communication, problem solving, reasoning, and connections. But a lot of the time, they have this question: How do you know that students know the basic skills or are able to compute? They have a sense that there's not a good balance." *Urban district mathematics supervisor*

> "Teachers ask, where do the basic skills get taught in relation to performance assessments? Before, during, after? Do performance assessments address the teaching of basic skills? In other words, and this is a question for a lot of parents, can we assume that a child that can perform on a high level on a performance assessment knows the basic skills?" *Director of assessment-based teacher program*

> "This is a more subjective way of assessing than multiple choice, in the sense that it relies on a subjective judgment. So a question teachers have is, is that fair? And of course, students have that question too. I think teachers can get around that by talking about the rubric before the assessment. On the other hand, . . . I have yet to write a rubric that I didn't need to revise once I saw the students' papers." *Teacher veteran of portfolio-scoring teams*

Here is an instance where a concern about assessment has aspects of more than one category to it: *consequence* (Will the students get shortchanged?) and *informational* (Where is the rigor in these new assessment systems?). Both aspects would need attention in the professional development.

Equity. The simplicity of the 4-part, cyclical diagram for the assessment process belies the complexity of assessment as a continuum of practice. On one end of the continuum, teachers must attend to students' individual interests and ways of thinking, and learn to incorporate portfolios and project work in such areas as data study, mathematical model of physical systems or phenomena, design of physical structures, management and planning analysis, pure mathematical investigations, and histories of mathematical ideas. (See, e.g., the performance standards categories developed by the New Standards Project, 1995.)

While portfolios and projects provide avenues for individual expression in assessment, there is another end to the continuum, where assessors must attend to things that society has deemed important and to standard ways of knowing. For example, society expects that, no matter their background, students will be able to perform well on tasks that relate to desired levels of literacy and numeracy in the citizenry, such as the task in Figure 12, administered to 17 year-olds in the National Assessment of Educational Progress (NAEP) and on which only three percent responded at the satisfactory level or better (Lindquist et al., 1995).

In between these two ends of the continuum are a range of individualized expressions of socially important ideas. This range appears to be growing in most classrooms, but it is especially wide in classrooms where teachers see a broad diversity in individual interests or, especially where many cultures are represented, they see a variety of socially important ideas. It becomes important for designers of professional development to look at assessment innovations through the lens of teachers' equity concerns. These concerns become especially relevant, and important to elicit, when judgments about task appropriateness and accessibility are at issue. For example, we have found it advantageous for teachers to discuss equity issues around the use of open tasks that invite students to explore and construct responses. Some teachers believe that some students require structured tasks all the time, and so should be protected from open tasks. This belief can, and should, be questioned and alternative perspectives should be considered.

> "I'm an advocate of open-ended problems because I think they allow for more equity. It's still a new experience for all students to have problems that could have multiple entry points and multiple solutions, problems that allow for sophisticated response or a basic response. If the problems are presented correctly, then everyone can have a stab at it. In contrast, if a problem depends on a certain technique, then if a student can't do it, that's it." *Urban high-school mathematics teacher*

Alternative assessment as an innovation is relatively young. Using the stages-of-concern lens on the concerns reported in our interviews, however, we can infer by the quantities of concerns in the management and consequences categories that the innovation is beginning to take root. At the same time, the educators we

---

Figure 12. A problem from NAEP

One plan for a state income tax requires those persons with incomes of $10,000 or less to pay no tax and those persons with income greater than $10,000 to pay a tax of 6 percent only on the part of their income that exceeds $10,000. A person's *effective* tax rate is defined as the percent of total income that is paid in tax.

Based on this definition, could any person's effective tax rate be 5 percent? Could it be 6 percent? Explain your answer. Include examples if necessary to justify your conclusions.

From the National Assessment of Educational Progress, as cited in Lindquist, Dossey, & Mullis, 1995.

interviewed report a range of concerns in the earlier categories, as well, implying that planning for assessment-based staff development should proceed from a concerns-based perspective, and allow participating teachers over time to begin reconsidering their perspectives on assessment, and to consider more powerful alternatives. The optimal staff-development event is one that addresses current concerns while it foreshadows future concerns.

In any case, it takes time to adopt and internalize new perspectives on assessment, and it takes considerable support. In the final section of the document, we advocate for actions that school administrators and others can take so that teachers get the necessary time and support.

V. Supporting and Extending Professional Development

"Policies, by themselves, don't impart new knowledge; they create the occasion for educators to seek new knowledge and turn that knowledge into new practice. Hence, the main link between policy and practice, in education reform, is professional development" (Elmore, 1996, p. 3).

Professional development focused on mathematics assessment is a necessary but not sufficient support for changes in classroom practice. The experience reflected in this document, both of the authors and of those practitioners interviewed, suggests that assessment-focused staff development can be a powerful lever for change *if* it is done in a thorough fashion, and in combination with other supports for change. In particular, the success of an assessment-focused staff-development program in effecting widespread changes in assessment practice depends on

- the systematic development of teacher expertise within a school or district around improved practice in assessment;

- the depth of support for assessment change that is expressed by district and building administrators and is expressed through the integration of assessment changes into other system efforts;

- the potential for the program to reach all the teachers in a building or all teachers in a district; and

- the depth of support and understanding in the community for the changes in assessment practice, demonstrated both by those citizens who have children in the schools and those who do not.

Driscoll and Bryant

For the administrator interested in supporting teachers in improving their classroom assessment practices, these criteria suggest a set of roles that extend beyond the design of effective professional development experiences.

Developing expertise of lead teachers

There is a growing knowledge base about classroom assessment in mathematics, and we recommend that a district or school should support lead teachers in efforts to understand and contribute to that knowledge base. Lead teachers should be supported in their experimentation with and reflection on improvements in classroom assessment practice.

> "I'm firmly convinced you need practicing teachers leading staff development. Start with a small group of teacher leaders, whom their peers respect, who will in time be able to get buy-in from other teachers in the field. That kind of buy-in doesn't come from efforts led by the superintendent. You have to build capacity among your teacher leaders. They have to be teachers that other teachers respect. You let them try things, and let them "sell" it— for lack of a better word—to other teachers.

> "You have got to build that capacity, it makes it much more believable. It's much more powerful. We used to rely on outside staff developers. . . . And now I think it's more powerful if it comes from teachers rather than outside experts. There's still a role for those folks in helping to develop the capacity with the teacher leaders, so that we have that capacity within the school building. We never really thought about it before, what teacher leaders need to know about staff development, what techniques and strategies." *Mathematics supervisor for large urban district in the west*

> "I think a good approach is teachers mentoring teachers. You need to start with the mentor, provide the release time so that person comes to believe in it and is good at it, and then the quickest way to get others involved is to have that person, the mentor, working with others." *A teacher who is a veteran of portfolio-scoring teams*

Our experience in assessment-focused groups makes us believe that expertise does not come without experimentation. And so an essential element of support is to nurture an experimental mindset among teachers and to provide them the latitude and time in their schools and districts to experiment.

Supporting lead teachers in working with others

Many teachers and administrators speak to the power of teacher-led staff development efforts. A cadre of well-informed and experienced lead teachers can work, over time, with a larger population of teachers, as a start to scaling up those changes in practice. Below are selected comments from those interviewed for this publication on the power of teachers leading professional development efforts.

> "You need to start instead with some people who are doing this stuff, start from the grassroots. Get your cadre of people, they're the ones that bring it to others, and then you're the support for that, but you're not the one stirring it up. Then movements get their ultimate validity from classroom use." *Mathematics supervisor, large urban district in the Midwest*

> "I would recommend a 'foot in the door' approach where you find or foster a couple of hotbeds of activity and build on and expand on that. You need to build it up with a grass roots base. If you call teachers all together, and tell them you've got the greatest thing since sliced bread, it's an external push, and it's going to fail." *Mathematics supervisor of large urban Midwestern district*

The words of these two interviewees, both large-district mathematics supervisors, speak volumes about the value of stepping aside and letting teacher expertise become the catalyst for the development of other teachers' expertise. Again, however, this kind of teacher leadership and change agency isn't self-activating nor is it self-supporting. Teachers who take the risk of engaging, challenging, and changing mindsets among their colleagues require the close support of administrators.

Aligning policies and practice

Classroom assessment practices need to consistent with other forms of assessment as well as system-wide policies. This may entail working toward alignment of district or state-mandated testing, protocols for school and teacher evaluation, and curriculum and instruction with the desired changes in assessment practice.

> "We can't do the traditional course, algebra 1, algebra 2, geometry, and add other subjects, and use performance tasks, and portfolios, and everything else. You have to couple the curriculum and the assessments. . . . I am convinced in many ways that we need to do this kind of assessment, but I am convinced that it can't be business as usual with just a change in the testing format." *Teacher who is a veteran of portfolio scoring teams*

> "In order to get things really moving in changing assessment in the classroom, there has to be some other leverage, like a state assessment, moving in the same direction. When CLAS (California Learning Assessment System) was moving, that helped us get things moving with teachers and schools. In other states, where testing is focused on computation, then the state test is an impediment. When a test is high stakes, like the state test, it has to be aligned with what you want to happen in the classroom." *Mathe-*

Something mentioned earlier bears repeating in this context. When teacher assessment groups are designed with a continuous-learning model of professional development, affording teachers regular cycling back to revise interests and learning goals, there are unprecedented opportunities for the teachers to broaden their perspectives on systemic thinking. As the teacher quoted earlier asked, "Now that we know how much our students don't know, what do we do instructionally?" In similar fashion, teachers will ask, "Now that I've bought into trying to incorporate more open-ended questioning into my teaching, where are the curriculum materials that can support this?" Piece by piece, in this fashion, a more systemically sound picture can evolve for teachers and administrators.

Communicating with the public

Changes in assessment are very public, particularly when they involve high stakes for students and schools. Ongoing communication with the public about changes in assessment practice is necessary, in order to develop a wide base of support among parents and other community members. Below, an administrator for the mathematics program in a large urban midwestern district shares concerns about public awareness, understanding and support.

> "My biggest concern right now is how do we educate the public. 32% of (our district's) citizens have kids in school. That means 68% of the public has no direct contact with the schools. So the question is, how do you get the word out? Our proficiency exam, when they printed it in the paper, opened people's eyes on what we were really expecting in the schools. Some people wrote into the paper saying, I couldn't do those problems, those are high expectations. Others said, wait, you're letting them use calculators?! The major support for schools, in terms of tax dollars, is uninformed about what goes on there. Why should dollars go into schools? These are issues in public awareness." *Urban mathematics supervisor in the midwest*

Luckily for teachers and administrators who want to embark on assessment-focused professional development, there is a growing knowledge base on building support among parents and other community members (NCTM, 1993). Public exhibitions of student work on high-quality mathematics tasks can make inroads. Parent meetings to discuss standards for performance are important. In general, it seems wise for teachers and administrators to take every opportunity to advocate for what they believe is important in mathematics assessment, and to invite, rather than discourage, discourse about and challenges to the values and principles they advocate.

References

1. Artin, M. (1995). Algebra at the college level. In C. Lacampagne (Ed.), *Proceedings of algebra initiative colloquium*. Washington, DC: U.S. Department of Education.

2. Balanced Assessment Project. For information contact Graduate School of Education, University of California, Berkeley, CA 94720.

3. Ball, D. (1994, November). *Developing mathematics reform: What don't we know about teacher learning—but would make good working hypotheses*. Paper prepared for conference on Teacher Enhancement in Mathematics K-6, Arlington, VA.

4. Barnett, C. et al. (Eds.), *Fractions, decimals, ratios, and percents: Hard to teach and hard to learn*. Portsmouth, NH: Heinemann.

5. Bryant, D. and Driscoll, M. J. (1998). *Exploring classroom assessment in mathematics: A guide for professional development*. Reston, VA: NCTM.

6. Clarke, D. J. (1993). Open-ended tasks and assessment: The nettle or the rose. Paper presented at the Research Presession of NCTM's 71st Annual Meeting.

7. Clarke, D. J. and Sullivan, P. A. (1992). The assessment implications of open-ended tasks in mathematics. In M. Stephens and J. Izard (Eds.), *Reshaping assessment practices: Assessment in the mathematical sciences under challenge* (pp. 161-179). Hawthorn, Australia: Australian Council for Educational Research.

8. Driscoll, M. J. (In preparation). Crafting a sharper lens: Classroom assessment in mathematics. In M. Solomon, *The diagnostic teacher: Revitalizing professional development*. New York: Teachers College Press.

9. Elmore, R. (1996, March). *Staff development and instructional improvement: Community District 2, New York City.* Paper prepared for the National Commission on Teaching and America's Future.

10. *Exemplars*, (1995, October). *3*(2). (http://www.exemplars.com, 271 Poker Hill Road, Underhill, VT 05489.)

11. Khattri, N. et al. (1995). How performance assessments affect teaching and learning. *Educational Leadership, 53*(3), 80-83.

12. Lambdin, D. V. , Kehle, P. E., and Preston, R. V. (Eds.). (1996). *Emphasis on assessment: Readings from NCTM's school-based journals.* Reston, VA: NCTM.

13. Lindquist, M. M., Dossey, J. A., and Mullis, I. V. S. (1995). *Reaching standards: A progress report on mathematics.* Princeton, NJ: Educational Testing Service.

14. Little, J. W. (1993). Teachers' professional development in a climate of educational reform. *Educational Evaluation and Policy Analysis, 15*(2), 129-151.

15. Loucks-Horsley, S. and Stiegelbauer, S. (1991). Using knowledge of change to guide staff development. In A. Lieberman and L. Miller, *Staff development for education in the 90's* (pp. 15-36). New York: Teachers College Press.

16. Loucks-Horsley, S., Stiles, K., and Hewson, P. (1996). Principles of effective professional development for mathematics and science education: A synthesis of standards. *NISE Brief, 1*(1).

17. Miller, B., Lord, B., and Dorney, J. (1994). *Staff development for teachers: A study of configurations and costs in four districts.* Newton, MA: Education Development Center.

18. National Assessment of Educational Progress. (1983). *The Third National Mathematics Assessment: Results, trends, and issues* (No. 13-MA-01). Denver, CO: Education Commission of the States.

19. National Council of Supervisors of Mathematics. (1996). *Great tasks and more!!: A sourcebook of camera-ready resources on mathematics assessment.* Golden, CO: Author.

20. National Council of Teachers of Mathematics. (1989). *Curriculum and evaluation standards for school mathematics.* Reston, VA: Author.

21. National Council of Teachers of Mathematics. (1991). *Professional standards for teaching mathematics.* Reston, VA: Author.

22. National Council of Teachers of Mathematics. (1993). *Communications handbook.* Reston, VA: Author.

23. National Council of Teachers of Mathematics. (1995). *Assessment standards for school mathematics.* Reston, VA: Author.

24. National Research Council. (1989). *Everybody counts: A report to the nation on the future of mathematics education.* Washington, DC: National Academy Press.

25. National Research Council. (1991). *For good measure: Principles and goals for mathematics assessment.* Washington, DC: National Academy Press.

26. National Research Council. (1993a). *Measuring up: Prototypes for mathematics assessment.* Washington, DC: National Academy Press.

27. National Research Council. (1993b). *Measuring what counts: A conceptual guide for mathematics assessment.* Washington, DC: National Academy Press.

28. Neill, M. et al. (1995). *Implementing performance assessments: A guide to school and system reform.* Cambridge, MA: FairTest.

29. New Standards Project. (1995). *Mathematics performance standards.* Washington, DC: National Center on Education and the Economy.

30. New Standards Project. (1997). *The New Standards mathematics reference examinations: Grades 4, 8, and 10.* Washington, DC: National Center on Education and the Economy.

31. Petit, M. (1992). *Getting started: Vermont mathematics portfolio—learning how to show your best!!* Cabot, VT: Cabot School.

32. Regional Educational Laboratory Network Program on Science and Mathematics. (1994). *A toolkit for professional developers: Alternative assessment.* Portland, OR: Northwest Regional Educational Laboratory.

33. Schifter, D. and Fosnot, C. (1993). *Reconstructing mathematics education.* New York: Teachers College Press.

34. Silver, E. A., Shapiro, L. J., and Deutsch, A. (1993). Sense making and the solution of division problems involving remainders: An examination of middle school students' solution processes and their interpretations of solutions. *Journal for Research in Mathematics Education, 24*(2), 117-135.

35. Stenmark, J. (Ed.). (1991). *Mathematics assessment: Myths, models, good questions, and practical suggestions.* Reston: NCTM.

36. Stiggins, R. (1988). Make sure your teachers understand student assessment. *Executive Educator, 10*(8), 24-30.

37. Thorpe, J. A. (1989). Algebra: What should we teach and how should we teach it? In S. Wagner and C. Kieren (Eds.), *Research issues in the learning and teaching of algebra* (pp. 11-24). Reston: NCTM.

38. Tsuruda, G. (1994). *Putting it together: Middle school math in transition.* Portsmouth, NH: Heinemann.

39. Van den Heuvel-Panhuizen, M. (1994). Improvement of (didactical) assessment by improvement of problems: An attempt with respect to percentage. *Educational Studies in Mathematics, 27*(4), 341-373.

40. Webb, N (Ed.). (1993). *Assessment in the mathematics classroom: 1993 yearbook.* Reston: NCTM.

41. Webb, N. (1997). *Criteria for alignment of expectations and assessments in mathematics and science education.* Madison, WI: National Institute for Science Education.

42. Wilson, L. (Ed.). (1995). Implementing the *Assessment standards for school mathematics*. *Mathematics Teacher* (a series beginning in 1995).

43. Wu, H. (1994). The role of open-ended problems in mathematics education. *Journal of Mathematical Behavior*, 13(1), 115-128.

Driscoll and Bryant

Appendix

The **Classroom Assessment in Mathematics (CAM) Network Project** (1991-1993) was an extension of the work done by the Urban Mathematics Collaboratives (UMC), and was a National Eisenhower Project (R168C10098-92) awarded by the Department of Education to Education Development Center (EDC). CAM piloted new approaches to staff development on the topic of mathematics classroom assessment. An overarching goal was to ground instructional change in teachers' knowledge of student understanding. The project took place in six UMC cities—Dayton, Memphis, Milwaukee, Pittsburgh, San Diego, and San Francisco—and was a collaborative effort among EDC staff, teams of middle-grades teachers in each site, and the six district mathematics supervisors. Over the course of CAM's two years, the teachers and administrators engaged in professional-development experiences aimed at building their capacities to use a variety of approaches to classroom assessment and to make appropriate interpretations of student work.

The **Assessment Communities of Teachers (ACT) Project** (1994-1997) extended the work of the CAM Network Project. It was a National Science Foundation teacher enhancement project (ESI-9353622) awarded to Pittsburgh Public Schools, with a technical-assistance contract to EDC. In ACT, the six CAM teams became leadership teams designing and implementing professional-development programs that focus on classroom assessment as a vehicle for changing teachers' classroom practice. The project was guided by the belief that professional development is most effective when it is ongoing, responsive to the needs of participants, content-rich, inquiry-based, and collaborative. EDC provided ACT teams with support in developing the knowledge, leadership skills, and materials to help them plan and implement effective professional-development programs focused on classroom assessment in mathematics. The ACT teams totaled approximately 60 teachers and administrators. Their district work, in turn, reached several hundred middle-grades teachers in the sites.

The **Leadership for Urban Mathematics Reform (LUMR) Project** (1994-1997) was a National Science Foundation teacher enhancement project (ESI-9353449) awarded to EDC, and took place in six UMC sites: Durham, Los Angeles, Milwaukee, St. Louis, San Diego, and Worcester. The project was designed to help the six districts develop the leadership capacities of middle and high school teachers, to develop ways to put that teacher leadership into the service of district mathematics reform, and to provide models of professional development that can support the kinds of teacher learning and capacity building that mathematics reform demands. Professional development in LUMR emphasized the development of algebraic thinking across middle- and high-school grades. In each site, two cohorts of teachers (each cohort an even mix of middle and high school teachers) spent two years apiece meeting monthly in study groups, wherein they worked on mathematics that highlighted algebraic thinking, analyzed student work, and developed leadership plans. Over the term of the project, approximately 200 teachers participated.